The Cornish Fishermen's Watch Night and Other Stories

Annonymous

[ZHINGOORA BOOKS]

This edition is published by
Zhingoora Books.

CONTENTS

- THE CORNISH FISHERMEN'S WATCH-NIGHT.

- THE BOOK THAT BROUGHT BAGS OF GOLD.

- THE MAN THAT EVERYTHING WENT AGAINST.

- ABOUT SCOLDING.

- THE FOOL AND THE BARON.

- THE TAILOR'S SPEECH.

- NOT A BIT AFRAID.

- TOLD AT A TUNNEL'S MOUTH.

- HARVEST HOME.

THE CORNISH FISHERMEN'S WATCH-NIGHT.

he old year was drawing to a close, indeed, it had not many hours to run, for the thirty-first of December had dawned upon the lonely Cornish village of Penwhinnock. It was a pouring wet day, and the wind was blowing so fiercely that the billows rolled and tossed as if some evil spirit, which could not rest, had taken possession of them. Penwhinnock overlooked the sea, being built upon a rocky promontory which commanded a splendid view of the Channel, and of any craft which might be nearing that part of the coast. The fishermen of the village were hardy, brave, stout, and strong; but whispers went abroad that they loved wrecking. It was said that battered and shipwrecked vessels had small chance if caught in the fearful gales which sometimes rose off that coast, and tempted the mariners to run for shelter to the bay, which proved after all a deceitful haven; and ugly tales were told of dead sailors, and of drowning men hurled back into the waters, on the principle that "dead men tell no tales," forgetting that, in the judgment to come, these would rise in swift witness against their murderers. Ostensibly the villagers of Penwhinnock gained their livelihood by fishing; but many a home contained valuables and wealth which had been obtained by this same practice of wrecking. Tourists and visitors looked askance at the Penwhinnock folk, and avoided their houses as if they had contained the plague, so that few strangers ever came among them or conversed with them.

There was one, however, who did not avoid them——would not, in fact. This person was the young minister, lately come into the neighbourhood, and as full of zeal and courage and self-sacrifice in his great Master's work as he was of health, hardy energy, and fearless pluck. Mr. Ernest Boyce was the very man to deal with those rough, semi-civilized, Cornish fishermen. Were they valiant, powerful, frank, and fearless? So was he; only in the service of a better Master. He was tall, well-built, and had eyes and ears as keen as they; but he was gentle, loving, forbearing, and considerate. A true gentleman and a true Christian, Mr. Boyce presented to those rough Cornish fishermen a pattern of true manliness. Their manliness consisted, for the most part, in being bold to commit sin; his, on the other hand, in being brave to serve God. They had talked once or twice of "frightening him off;" but his brave, loving, outspoken, disinterested Christian honesty of purpose had disarmed them, and caused their hostility to slumber, though it had not yet died away. Penwhinnock was situated some eight miles or so from his residence, but very regularly every week Mr. Boyce rode over there to hold the appointed service. This service was always held in the evening, and Mr. Boyce noticed with a sharp, quick intelligence, that while he had a fair audience on fine, warm, mild, or quiet evenings, he had scarcely anybody to hear him if the evening turned out stormy, rough, or dark; and being a gentleman of quick perceptions, he lost no time in solving this problem. As to the solution at which he arrived he said but little, but ever after that he ordered his dealings with the fisher-folk accordingly,——that is to say, if the afternoon betokened "big guns," he would ride over to Penwhinnock early, and visit freely at the fishermen's cottages, inviting, persuading, entreating, and almost "compelling them to come in" to the meeting. And now that the last day of the old year had dawned, amid storm, wind, rain, and roaring of billows, there seemed but little doubt that he would be over as usual, visiting among the villagers, and charging them to attend the "Watch-night service." For there was a watch-night service to be held in the accustomed meeting-place, which was a large empty cottage adjoining a farmhouse, and Mr. Boyce was to preside.

This was what the Penwhinnock men were discussing as they stood around some of the largest fishing-boats, dragged up on the beach for safety, and watched the gathering storm. The wind was blowing "big guns" then, and the rain was pelting fiercely down upon the bare, rugged rocks, and the mean, small cottages which formed the dwellings of the fishermen, and lined each side of the long straggling village street. It would have appeared to most landsmen as if the weather could not be much worse; but to the experienced eyes of the fishermen the night promised worse things——worse things to many an ill-fated mariner——but in the judgment of those hardy, cruel men it might bring to them "a good catch." This meant a brave ship being wrecked, flung hopelessly and helplessly upon the dreadful rocks, decoyed there by false lights, and lured into the jaws of death; it meant, too, robbery, pillage, cruelty, and, not seldom, *murder*!

"What do you think of the night?" inquired Bob Trevannion of Will Lowry.

"Think! Why, many a good ship will go down before another year dawns. That's what I think. And parson thinks so, too, I guess, for see, here he is!"

Turning their faces towards the place indicated by the speaker, the group saw Mr. Boyce coming through the rain quietly, on his stout, sure-footed pony.

"Eh!" said Hugh Hoskyns, a brawny six-footer. "I guess we'll have to attend the cottage to-night."

"So we shall, man," replied Will Lowry; "but we shall leave in time to do a good night's work, if all be well. The *Fleur-de-lis* is due up about this part toward morning, and our mates will be ready about on the hills in good time. But we must needs go to parson's 'Watch-night,' or he'll be poking his nose into our fun, and spoiling it."

"Seems to me you've laid your plans well but I shouldn't wonder if parson isn't as deep," slily retorted Bob Trevannion. "He's up to all of it most as much as the wreckers themselves."

"Never mind if he is. He'll not know anything this time, for we've put up the women and children to it; and though he may ride about this afternoon, visiting one and another, he'll not get anything. We shall go to his meeting right enough, then we'll wish him 'good-bye,' and while he's trotting off home and out of the storm, we'll look after our own business. Never fear!"

And the men chuckled again at thinking of their sagacity in outwitting Mr. Boyce. It showed the hold which one determined servant of the Lord could obtain over those wicked, resolute men, by his calm, fearless faith and outspoken fidelity. They could not plan their wrecking expedition as of old, but must consider first how to blind and deceive him. But he was more '"cute" than they dreamed. Mr. Boyce had not lived thirty years in the world without opening both eyes and ears, and he read, by the embarrassed silence of the children and the prevaricating, evasive replies of the women, that some business was on hand, either wrecking or smuggling——for the Penwhinnock folk were smugglers, too——of which he was to be kept ignorant. But the fisher folk had reckoned without their host.

Mr. Boyce took a cup of tea here, and a broiled fish there, on his peregrinations through the village that evening, so strengthening himself for his night's vigil. There were sick folk to be seen, inquirers to be instructed, families to be catechized, and sundry other duties appertaining to his office to be performed; and, to do the people justice, they were never stingy or rude to him. Open-handed hospitality was generally the rule towards Mr. Boyce; but, as generally happens, the thing was so overdone, and he was so condoled with in reference to his midnight journey on this particular afternoon, that he felt sure that some mischief was intended. And the women and children unconsciously confirmed all his suspicions. So Mr. Boyce laid his plans.

The service was to begin at ten o'clock that evening. As I said, it was to be held in a large unoccupied cottage adjoining a farmhouse. The thin partition between the two downstair rooms had been removed, so that a pretty fair number could assemble in the place "where prayer was wont to be made." The people came trooping in in great numbers, considering the weather, until nearly all the able-bodied men and lads, together with many women and girls, were present. As usual, the service was opened with singing, in which Will Lowry and Hugh Hoskyns joined with apparent good will. Then Mr. Boyce read and prayed, after which another hymn was given out. Then he preached a sermon on the flight of time, and, not sparing the vices which reigned in Penwhinnock, besought his hearers tenderly and affectionately to remember that another year of their mortal probation was slipping away from them, that each left one less to live, and, though so near its end, they could not know certainly that they would ever see the commencement of the year just about to dawn. He reminded them of their mercies, as numerous as the sands of the sea, and of their sins, if possible, more numerous still. He besought them to examine themselves in the fading hour of that last day of another year, and to humble themselves before God for their manifold offences committed during that year. As he depicted the great meeting around the judgment-seat, there to give account, each one for himself, of the deeds committed during this and every preceding year, his hearers looked grave. There are solemn hours in the life of the most wicked man and woman upon earth, and this hour was a solemn one in the lives of those fishermen. They sat and listened most attentively, while some, I doubt not, half wished that they had never engaged either in wrecking or smuggling.

The sermon was ended, and it being about a quarter to twelve, Mr. Boyce gave out a hymn, thus commencing the short prayer-meeting which he had announced as following the sermon. During the singing of that hymn Mr. Boyce very coolly stepped to the door, locked it, and put the key in his pocket. As the strains of the singing died away, the voices of Hugh Hoskyns and Bob Trevannion were heard in no gentle tones threatening the preacher with violence if he did not give up the key, so as to afford them free egress and ingress. "They were not going to stay there all night, to suit his fancies," they said, and endeavoured to assert their independence of all laws, human and Divine. Two or three minutes passed in this way, and then Mr. Boyce spoke plainly.

"I shall not keep you here all night, friends; but you will not leave this watch-night service yet awhile. I believe that a blessing is coming; I feel sure of it, and the greatest sinners could not find in their hearts to refuse a blessing from heaven. Could you? And you know that you need a blessing! Most of all, you need the blessing of forgiveness!"

"Yes, that may sound all very well for you to preach, as a parson," spoke up Bob Trevannion; "but I don't know as we want so much preaching just now. Here we've been for nearly two mortal hours listening to your service, and I say it's precious hard if you won't let us out now."

"You will not leave yet, Bob Trevannion," coolly replied Mr. Boyce. "And, beside that, we are just entering upon the last five minutes of the dying year. You remember, too, that my announcement for the watch-night service informed you that we should *watch in* the new year. So, according to that announcement, your time is not up yet. We will spend the last five minutes in prayer, silent prayer, each one for himself and herself. And may the Lord pour you down such a blessing that there shall not be room enough to receive it."

At this the assembly again grew quiet; they could not for very shame refuse to fulfil the conditions of the service. The men sat still, moody, silent, and jealously afraid of Mr. Boyce; but whether they prayed I cannot say. Some of the women appeared to be in fervent supplication, with one or two of the older men. Perhaps they were beginning to see, although but dimly, that the wild, lawless life of their sons, husbands, and brothers was ill befitting "those who had to give an account of the deeds done in the body," and to whom the knell of every passing year told of added sins, with lessened opportunities for repentance. Mr. Boyce bent his head low in earnest pleading with God on behalf of this rough, sinful assembly; pleading with tears for "a present blessing," even the descent of the Holy Spirit. And through it all the storm howled and roared, and the sea tossed its restless foaming billows, as though hungry for the lives of those who were out that night upon her broad bosom. The rain beat with terrific force against the windows, while even the old trees creaked and bent beneath the power of the wind. So passed the last five minutes of that memorable year.

Twelve o'clock! There were no church bells to ring out the hour, and to welcome with their musical peal the dawning of the new year. But Mr. Boyce arose, and said,——

"Friends, it is twelve o'clock!... Now it is five minutes past. I wish you all a very happy, a very blessed, new year! The old year is gone into eternity, with all its faults, its sins written down in God's book of remembrance. This new year comes to you full of mercy. Its record is now spread open before you like a fair white page, upon which you may inscribe anything you like. But you will not make any good entries there unless God's grace, helps you. And in order to pray for that grace, let us bend before God's throne a little longer."

"I vote that we've had enough of your praying for one night, Mr. Boyce," spoke up Hoskyns. "We've sat out your watch-night service now, and we want to be going. So I shall go, and my mates too, or we'll know the reason why." He made a move towards the door as he spoke.

"You can't go out of that door," said Mr. Boyce. "It is locked, and I have the key in my pocket."

"Then hand it over, if you please," said Hugh, roughly; "or I shall be at the pains to make you. And it's not worth while, mister."

"You say rightly, it is not worth while," said Mr. Boyce. "God is in this place. He knows the very secret thoughts of your hearts; He is at this moment noting your secret intentions of doing evil. Will you dare to brave God's anger, Hugh?"

"I don't want to be trifled with," rejoined Hugh. "I am not a child, to be frightened. When I say I'll do a thing, I mean it; and I've said I'll leave this meeting."

"Listen, Hugh Hoskyns," said Mr. Boyce, solemnly. "God will not be trifled with. He says, 'He, that being often reproved, hardeneth his neck, shall suddenly be destroyed, and that without remedy.' He says, too, 'Behold, now is the accepted time, now is the day of salvation.' Will you spurn all these warnings? Will you say that you do not need a blessing? Will you rush away to sin——right from the mercy-seat? Think again, I entreat you. I want to do you good, not to harm you. I will not believe that you intend evil towards me, knowing, as you do, that I wish nothing but good to you. As I said before, I simply want to do you good. Else why should I ride over to this place every week, and work among you, were it not for that? Does any one else care enough about you to do that?"

"No, no! that they don't," were the murmured responses. "We're much obliged to you, Mr. Boyce, for your interest in us. But it seems very hard laws to be shut up here against our wills."

"I won't keep you very long, only long enough for the blessing to come, the blessing which I feel sure *is coming*. And consider what a dreadful thing it is for you to slight that blessing. Why, how do you know what will happen? God's voice is abroad, on the face of the waters, and in nature. Suppose you were going home through this hurricane of wind and rain, and one of those large old trees were to fall before you got clear of the fields, where would your soul be, if the tree fell upon you? Answer me that question——or, no, answer it to God. And do it *honestly* to Him." At this they sat still, cowed into silence.

The wind roared and howled still, as Mr. Boyce was speaking; and just at that moment a loud crash was heard. The farmer to whom the cottage belonged went out to see what was the matter; and to his astonishment——for the rest were too frightened to move——he found that one of the large old trees standing near had been blown down, and had only by a short distance cleared the pathway leading to the cottage. Singular to say, God had permitted the winds to do His will just at that moment, and confirmed in a most remarkable manner the words of His servant. As the old farmer returned to the cottage and reported what had happened, awe fell upon the people. Even Hugh Hoskyns and Bob Trevannion, as they realized how near they had been to death, sat still and shuddered. Had not Mr. Boyce been firm, they would at that very time have been in the path of the fallen tree; and once under its dreadful trunk, where would their souls have been? They felt that their portion would have been in *hell*. It was no use to shirk the matter; for, look at it which way they would, they felt that they were not fit for heaven, and, not being fit for heaven, their place would have been found in *the lost world*.

As I said, awe fell upon the little assembly, and many knees bent in prayer that night which had not so bent for years. No more was said about the watch-night service, or their desire to leave it, but one after another, those rude, rough fishermen *prayed*, in broken, uncouth petitions, for pardon. The Spirit descended, and strove mightily with the people, until five or six of the roughest, including Bob Trevannion and Hugh Hoskyns, were found crying for mercy; and over many more of them Mr. Boyce could rejoice ere the meeting broke up, because, like Saul of Tarsus, it could be said of each of them, "*Behold, he prayeth.*"

That watch-night service was the commencement of a great revival in the village. A church was built, and the little believing community gathered together in one body. Wrecking almost entirely disappeared; and smuggling, although it took longer time to make it die, vanished gradually before the clearer light of Gospel truth. The *Fleur-de-lis* escaped her threatened fate, through the fact of being detained on her voyage somewhat longer than was anticipated by the wreckers of Penwhinnock. Hugh Hoskyns, Will Lowry, Bob Trevannion, and all the rest, grew to delight more in things "honest, pure, just, true, lovely, and of good report;" so that those things in which they once delighted became a shame to them. No better friends had Mr. Boyce from that time than those who had threatened him with violence during that ever-memorable watch-night service.

THE BOOK THAT BROUGHT BAGS OF GOLD.

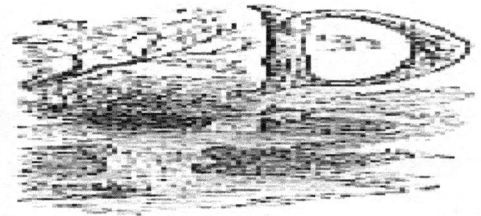

uring the war between France and England a frigate sailed from a South American port, on board of which were a Brazilian widow named Maria da Silva and her child Francisca. Her husband had been in the service of the British Government; she herself had become a Protestant, and was now driven by persecution from her home. She was coming to Europe in the hope of finding a brother, her only surviving relative, who had preceded her some years before. The poor woman's health was failing when she came on board. Anxiety and sorrow soon completed the work which disease had begun, and her death drew near. The sailors were very kind to her in their rough way, especially Wat Connor, who was an old messmate of her husband's, and had gone through many hardships and dangers with him.

Feeling that her end was near, Maria da Silva expressed to Wat her solicitude respecting her little Francisca, so soon to be left an orphan amongst strangers. Wat at once promised that little "Sisker Silver," as he called her, should never want a friend as long as he lived. The dying woman raised her eyes in grateful acknowledgment of his kindness, and said——

"I have nothing to leave her but this little money. I have a Bible: if you will promise me that she shall learn to read it, I shall die in peace."

"She sha'n't want for nothing while I can get it; and as to the book——all right—— when she's old enough, I'll see to her tackling it."

"And will you read it, too?" said she, earnestly.

"I would if I could," said Wat, bluntly; "if it would do you any good, or her either."

"Not for her nor me, but for yourself," she said. "Depend on it, kind, dear friend, it will be better to you than bags of gold. This Book helped my husband to bear sickness, meet death, and submit to leave me alone in the world; it has supported me under his loss, and enabled me to see nothing but love in all the troubles I have had; and now, trusting in its promises, I am not afraid to die——not afraid to leave my child. Do believe what I say, learn to read, and make this precious Book your friend——oh, *do*!"

"Well, I will——thank'ee," said Wat, taking the book with respect. "I can't say no fairer."

Very soon after this the widow was lowered among the waves. Wat immediately took possession of her purse and clothes, which he made into a little bundle for the child; and having stowed that and the Bible safely away, he went to work with his charge, with whom he had become very familiar.

With a gravity, importance, and fatherly tenderness, Wat regularly attended to what he called "rigging little Sisky." Perfectly indifferent to the jokes of his companions, he went as methodically through all the ceremonies of the nursery as if he had been "groom of the chamber" or "mistress of the robes."

"Where's Wat?" was asked, one morning, when he was busy with Sisky's toilette.

"Oh, he's with the child," said a messmate.

"What, topping and tailing his gooseberry?" was the reply.

From that time "Sisky" was better known as "Wat's gooseberry" than by any other name; and Wat himself, being highly diverted with the joke, took to calling her Gooseberry, declaring it was a deal more English-like than "Sisky."

When the voyage ended, Wat, who had no relations but an old grandmother, was rather at a loss what to do with his charge, who was now about six years old; but after a little consideration, he mounted a stage-coach which ran from the port where he had landed to the place where his grandmother lived.

Nothing could exceed the delight of the child at all she saw. After the tedious life on board ship, the green hedges and trees, the fields, the cottages, the pretty sights all along the road, made her clap her hands with joy. Wat was happy, too; and if anything could have made him more light-hearted than he was, it was the high spirits and rejoicing of his little Gooseberry.

Some years had passed since he had been to see his grandmother. Was she alive? He looked out rather anxiously at the places he passed, till the coach came to the top of a green lane, with an alder hedge on each side.

"Into port, captain," he cried, checking the coachman; "here's our landing-place." And dismounting, he took Gooseberry on his shoulder and the bundles under his arm, and went down the lane.

One cottage——two——three——he passed, but at last he stopped at a pretty, though very humble dwelling, with flowers trained round the door. *That* was the house. There was the old boat summer-house that his father had made, and there was his granny knitting in the garden.

The old lass was well pleased to see him, and he was heartily glad to find her "all right and tight," as he said, and hugged her as if she had been his mother.

After a few words of pleasure and surprise, granny turned towards Gooseberry, who was staring with her great black eyes on all before her.

"What, married, my lad? and brought me thy little one?" she said.

Wat told the story, and taking up her bundle, he added, "When she's able to be put forward in life, I shall lay out the money on her, and give her them clothes; but till then I shall look to her like my own."

Granny remonstrated. The workhouse was the proper place. He might marry, and then what could he do with this child? This was right and reasonable, as Wat allowed, but he affirmed that it was "righter and more reasonabler" that he should keep his promise. Granny, finding him positive, consented to let Gooseberry live with her; and though he had a misgiving that she wouldn't have a lively time of it, yet he felt she would be safe for the present. So he emptied his pockets most liberally of pay and prize-money, and gave the child into her care.

"Ye see, mother," he said, the night before he left, "I am bound to have her learned to read, and to read this Book; and I'm bound, likewise, to learn to read the Book myself, seeing as I promised I'd do both them things. Now nobody can be at sea and on shore at the same time; and by that rule, how can I leave the Book for her, and take it for myself?"

Wat's puzzle was set at rest by Granny's telling him that she would teach Gooseberry out of her Bible, which would be the same thing, as all Bibles were exactly alike.

"I reckon so," he said, with a perplexed look, comparing Sisky's with the old baize-covered one on the settle. "But there's a lot of signs and marks in this 'un," pointing to red ink notes on the margin, and underlinings of several passages.

Granny inspected it, and shook her head.

"I don't know nought of the writing, lad, but the printing is the same as mine," she said; and reading the opening of Genesis from both the Books, she succeeded in persuading him that they were one and the same, except the red ink.

"Heave to, then!" he cried. "I'll have Sisky's; it's trimmer to haul about than yonder woolly-backed one, and I'll try to spell it out when I get aboard again."

To say truth, Wat had found his engagement to take care of the child less troublesome than his promise to learn to read. He had got on till now extremely well without any knowledge of that art, and he felt a hearty repugnance to a job he knew so little about.

It was not long before Wat got a ship, and sailed again. The parting between him and Sisky was a sorer trial than he had looked for. Granny was not so sensitive, and couldn't understand how he should care to leave a little one like that, who had no call on him, more than his own old grandmother whom he had not seen for so long. Sisky openly rebelled at the idea of being left behind. When he had really gone the child was for a time inconsolable. Her only consolation seemed to be to sit in the old boat summer-house, where she could see the sea, and watch every vessel that glided by, hoping, till the hope faded away, that her dear "Daddy Wat" would come back again.

Granny left her very much to her own devices. She fed her and clothed her; and, that done, there was but one thing more she had engaged for——to teach her the Bible. This she tried very earnestly to do; but Sisky didn't like her, and wouldn't learn, and gave her so much trouble, that, finding the funds sufficient, she put her in charge of Mary Keythorn, an excellent young woman, who supported her aged mother by teaching the village children.

"She's as wigglesome and unsettled as ever a sailor on land, or a fish out of the sea," said Granny, as she delivered her over to Mary; "but Wat made me promise she should learn to read this Bible, and I'm bound to keep my word."

Gooseberry pricked up her ears at this. She had never been told it was Daddy Wat's desire she should read; but now she knew it, she went to work with her whole heart, and what with fair abilities, a thorough good will, and a gentle and patient teacher, she soon became a pretty good scholar.

Wat was not quite so prosperous in his studies. Once fairly on board again, he seldom thought of Sisky's Book, and when he did, it made him uneasy. He wished in his heart he had never made the promise.

The ship had been running before a gale for some hours, and everything portended a storm. The ship was nearing a coast where many a wreck had happened. All that seamanship could do had been done, and they were now waiting the result.

One of the passengers, with a Book in his hand, said calmly, as Wat passed him,——

"Do you think there is danger?"

"Lots," said Wat.

The man, after a moment's pause, reopened his Book and read on.

"You take it very comfortable," said Wat.

"I am not afraid. I can depend on this promise," said the man, pointing to his Book.

Wat shook his head.

"I can't take in that, worse luck, master. May be yourn's the same as this," said Wat, taking Sisky's Bible from his pocket, where he always kept it when his conscience was troubled, as if to pacify it with a sort of showing his good intentions.

The man looked attentively at the Bible, while Wat, in a few words, told him its history, and confessed his neglect, which he had never more truly lamented.

A sudden call from the mate made him leave the book in the man's hands, and it was not till after two or three hours of hard work that he returned with the joyful news that the danger was past.

"The Lord be praised!" said the man.

"Poor Sisky's mother used to talk about the Lord," said Wat. "She told me reading that Book would be better than bags of gold to me."

"So it will. Let me teach you," said the man.

"With right good will, my hearty," said Wat; "and I'll pay you with part of my 'bacca or rum now, or money when I get my pay."

"My good fellow," said the man, "I want no pay. I am greatly in your debt already. This Book belonged to my sister; it was all she had of my father's goods. He had nothing to leave, but he told her she would find it better than bags of gold. She did. You have only to read it, and you will find the same."

"Well, that's curious enough," said Wat. "And how came it you never looked after her and little Sisky?"

"I was in Europe; I have been long away from home. Until I heard your story, and saw from this Book who the mother and the child you spoke of were, I did not know her history."

The stranger told him further that he was desirous to provide for his sister's child, and after he had been home and arranged all his family affairs, he would return to England, and take his niece under his protection, and, as far as he could, repay him for his goodness to her.

Wat declared that he could not part with his little Gooseberry, but he gratefully set to work to learn to read. As he learned, Da Silva, whose heart was penetrated with the truth, kept earnestly endeavouring to present it acceptably to his pupil; and as the letter of the Word entered his mind, the grace of God blessed it to his true conversion.

The voyage ended, he lost no time in going to his Granny's. There he found her, as usual, knitting in the garden.

After greetings were passed, he asked for Sisky, and hearing she was at school, went to fetch her. He made his best sailor's bow to Miss Mary in somewhat a shy style, for he had once tried to induce her to look with favour on him, but, for some undeclared reason, she had not consented. The meeting between him and the child was very joyous. She held his jacket tight, as if to prevent his again giving her the slip.

"Hear me read, Daddy Wat! Mistress has taught me! I can read quite fast!" she cried.

"All right. The next thing is to understand it, and then you'll be all right for sea," said Wat.

Sisky opened the Bible and began to read. It happened to be a place that Wat knew pretty well, so he was well pleased to prompt her now and then, and, moreover, to give her a concise commentary, more to Mary's pleasure and edification than little Sisky's, who was impatient at the interruption.

Before they left, Wat felt that Mary looked more kindly on him than she had done in old days. She was still free. He was not long in coming to a point when he was clear upon its propriety. So he, quite suddenly, a few days after his return, asked her without much "roundabouts," as he said, "whether she'd the same objections to sail along with him as she had once manifested." Mary honestly answered *no*. She told him her objections before had not arisen from any want of liking for him; but she said, "I knew that I was but a weak and ignorant Christian, and I was afraid, from the way you talked, you were not one at all; and I dared not venture on such a marriage."

"I'm a poor hand at it now," he said, with great humility.

"Poor enough I am," she answered; "but so long as we are of one mind we shall help one another on. I feel safe about that."

Poor Wat! Every year of his married life brought him, as he said, "fuller bags of gold;" for a sweeter, kinder, better wife, man never had than Mary made him.

The peace came. Wat left the service, but his character was so good that he had no difficulty in getting a place in the coast-guard; and in his cottage by the sea he maintained wife and children, old granny, and little Gooseberry, who, however, was little no longer. In his spare time he cultivated a bit of ground, and this with his pay kept all comfortable. Still his family was increasing, and food was dear: money went faster and faster. "Never mind," said Wat, "godliness with contentment is great gain."

One day when he came home from duty, he found all out, the door locked, and the key in the thatch, as usual. He went in, and on the table was a canvas bag. He opened it, expecting to find beans for sowing, but out tumbled Spanish dollars. While he was wondering, Sisky, who had been to look for him, ran in. The tale was soon told. Her uncle had come for her, and had put that bag on the table for her Daddy Wat.

Philip da Silva, having settled all his affairs, had resolved to live in England, all his near relations having moved away from his native place or died. He purchased a small property in the neighbourhood, taking care that Wat and his wife should share in his prosperity. Little Sisky, whom he looked on as his child, helped him heartily as years went on to forward the happiness and interests of her foster-father and his family.

"Mary dear," said Wat, many and many a time, "what blessings have come to me through getting this Book! Bags of gold! why, what are they to having you for a wife? and, above all, to the hope I've got of being pardoned for all my sins, and received into heaven when I die?"

THE MAN THAT EVERYTHING WENT AGAINST.

tell you," said poor Ned, angrily, "everything has gone against me all my life long. If I had had other people's chances I should have been a different sort of a man, and you wouldn't have had to come looking me up here. But I never had a chance, and so what's the use of talking?"

Ned Bean was one of my neighbours; but at this time he was lodged in the jail of the next town——and dear lodgings they were likely to prove to him. He was an old man: his scanty white hair, his rough, unshorn chin, his haggard, thin face, now flushed with momentary excitement, his rough countryman's garb, dirty and neglected——all this and more made him an object for pity. A volcano of wrath was pent up in that old man's bosom, striving for vent.

He had been committed only a few days before for brutally misusing his poor old wife——half killing her, in fact, in a fit of ungoverned fury. The case was too serious to be disposed of by the magistrate before whom he had been at first taken, and who had sent it to the higher county sessions.

I had the day before visited the injured woman, who lay groaning from the effects of her husband's savage assault; and it was at her request, or rather her earnest prayer, that I went the next day to see the unhappy prisoner.

"No," said he once more, when I was considering what further to say, seeing that his old wife's kind and forgiving messages, which I had delivered, had wrought no softening effect on his mind——"No; I never had a chance; and there's the end on't."

"How is it that you never had a chance, neighbour?" I asked, as kindly as I could, for it occurred to me that if poor old Bean were encouraged to tell his grievances, I might be better able to put in a word or two afterwards.

"How is it?" said he. "Why, haven't I been a poor man all my life? and when a man is poor everything goes against him, doesn't it?"

"I am not sure that it does, neighbour Bean. Some have not found it so," said I; not adding, however, as I might have done, that there were other poor men in the world, who were not in the habit of battering their wives, as he had done.

He had always been a lone thing in the world——so he said; he had never known father or mother, brother or sister. He had been brought up in the parish workhouse, to which he had been taken when a helpless baby; and when old enough to do a bit of work he was set to that. According to his statement he was badly used by everybody in the house, and was glad enough to get sent out to service as a waggoner's boy at a farm. But there he wasn't treated much better, for he was knocked about by the waggoner till he couldn't stand it any longer, so he ran away. There were bills stuck about the country, describing him, and offering a reward to any one for taking him up and bringing him back again. "But they forgot that I could read the bills as well as they could," said poor old Bean, with a chuckle.

"But why did they take the trouble to post bills about you?"

"They said I had taken something that wasn't mine——the waggoner's money," old Ned explained, with a little reluctance.

"I suppose you were not caught and taken back to your place?"

"No; I took care to get far enough away, and went into the country with a set of tramps. I got work in a hop garden, and when hopping was over, master, seeing I was a likely sort of a young chap, offered to take me on, and give me regular work."

"Well, that was kind, at all events," I remarked. "Don't you think so, neighbour?"

"Oh, I don't know as to that," said the old man; "if he hadn't thought I was worth my money, he wouldn't have took to me. Every man for himself, you know."

"Well, anyhow, in being for himself, your new master was for you as well, I think."

Bean went on to say he slaved and slaved, and got his pay, but not much thanks. But he couldn't do better; and so he stopped, and went on slaving "lots of years," till he "was a man upgrown." Then he got married.

"To the same poor old creature whom you so badly misused the other day, and who has sent you her forgiving messages by me?"

"Ah, yes, well; just as you like, sir; only she wasn't old then. That was forty years gone by."

"You have lived together forty years, then? and have always been poor, as I suppose, neighbour?"

"You are safe to say that, master," he replied, sharply. "How is a man to get rich on twelve or fourteen shillings a week, and sometimes out of work, and a family to bring up?"

"Not very likely to get rich——especially when he spends much of his spare time and a large part of his earnings at the beershop," I ventured to say.

"What's that to——to anybody?" asked Bean, fiercely. It seemed as though he meant, "What's that to *you*?" but he stopped short at the word. "It was my own money I spent," he added.

"And what became of your sons and daughters——poor things?" I asked him.

"They went to the bad, mostly. There was Ned, the oldest——he took to poaching, and was sent across the water for knocking a gamekeeper about. Then there was Tom; he went for a soldier, and I never heard of him afterwards. The girls got married, and didn't make much of that. The only one that did any good was Joe, and he got a place in London, or somewhere; but he went against me, like everybody else. The last time I saw him he had a good coat on his back, and good shoes on his feet, and money in his pocket; but he wouldn't give his old father a penny. He told me if he did I should only get drunk with it. A pretty sort of a son that, sir!"

"But about your wife, neighbour. You cannot deny that you are in the habit of treating her roughly; and that last affair, you know, which has brought you here——
——"

"She shouldn't have given me so much tongue," said the old man. "She is always giving me tongue, she is!"

"Well, neighbour," said I, when poor Bean had come to an end of his story and his complaints, "I really am very sorry for you. I can plainly see, from everything you have told me, that you have been badly used all your life, up to the present time."

"Ah, I thought you would say so when you came to know the rights of it," said my poor neighbour, suddenly brightening up a little.

"You have had one enemy in particular who has always set himself against you. I think I happen to know who it is," I said.

"More than one; lots of them," poor old Ned protested.

"Let us stick to that one," I went on. "I'll tell you about him. To begin at the beginning, it was he who would not permit you to get any good out of the teaching you had when you were a poor little orphan boy. It was he, only you did not know it, who sent you wandering over the country as a tramp and vagabond, when you might have gone on comfortably and respectably with your first master. It was he who took away your character and branded you as a thief. It was this same enemy of yours who, when you grew older, sent you to the beershop, when you would otherwise have been industriously at work, or sitting at home quietly and happily with your wife and children. It is he who set your children against you, and drove them, as you say, 'to the bad,' my poor neighbour. You don't know it, but this same person has destroyed your peace and pleasure in your own house, and has robbed you of pounds and pounds, which would have helped to make you comfortable in your old age."

"I wish I knew who he is!" exclaimed the old man, rousing himself excitedly.

"I will tell you, neighbour; but I have one thing more to say about this enemy——I have great reason to believe that he is doing a good deal to shorten your life."

"You don't say that, sir!" cried the poor man, with some signs of alarm. "But now you speak of it," he continued, "I have felt sometimes as if I was being poisoned."

"Ah, no doubt. Well, that was your enemy's doing. And not to make a longer story of it, the man I am speaking of has destroyed every chance you ever had of getting on—

—and you have had chances——he has upset your poor old wife's temper, and urged her on to give you so much tongue, as you say."

"I can't think who you can mean, or what you are talking about, sir," said my old neighbour, ponderingly.

"The name of the man who has done you all this mischief is Edward Bean, commonly called Tipsy Ned. Do you know him?"

For a moment or two poor Ned did not speak, but sat looking at me savagely. Then the muscles of his face worked convulsively, and his eyes were slowly withdrawn from my face, and looked down on the prison floor. Then he muttered, "I reckon you are right, sir."

I knelt down and prayed with and for my poor old neighbour before I left the jail; and that was the last I saw of him. He was soon afterwards tried, and condemned to six months' imprisonment for the assault on his wife, but he did not live out the term. His constitution was shattered by previous habits. He was taken ill, and died in the infirmary of the county prison.

The circumstances I have related have nearly passed from the memory of those in the village where he once lived; but I have revived the story, "to point a moral," though it may not "adorn a tale."

ABOUT SCOLDING.

"I'd go and break stones on the road rather than be sitting indoors doing nothing, Will," I heard Mrs. Howland say as I was walking up to the cottage door. The words were spoken sharply, and the tone was in a high pitch.

"Ho, ho," thought I, "if the wind is in that quarter, perhaps I had better make my call at another time;" and I hesitated for a moment. But as I really had some business with William Howland, and as I had got so far, I made up my mind not to turn back.

William Howland is a good man, I verily believe; but I am bound (if I must speak out) to say that he is not——well, not to write too strongly——not over fond of hard work. He has a wife and family dependent on his exertions, and he had recently, two or three weeks previous to this call of mine, lost a place of regular employment, fifteen shillings a week wages, because he could not or would not get up soon enough in the morning.

The case was this. He had, three months before (after a good deal of knocking about, sometimes in work, and rather oftener out of it), applied to a neighbouring farmer for a situation then vacant on the farm.

"I am afraid you won't suit me, Howland," said the farmer; "but, as you say you want work, I'll try you. But you'll understand, I shall expect you at your post by a quarter before six in the morning."

"That's early, sir," said Will.

"Yes, a quarter of an hour before the regular time, I know. But you will have to be timekeeper to the other men, who begin work at six; and it will be proper for you to be on the farm before they come. However, that's the condition on which I shall employ you. Take the place or leave it."

Howland decided that, upon the whole, it was best to take it, which he did; and for a few weeks he managed to be at his post at the appointed time. Then he began to slacken, sometimes being five minutes behind, sometimes ten, until at last he seemed to settle in his mind that six o'clock was the proper time to commence his day's work; and he did not always stick to that. The consequence was he lost his place; and after that, up to the time of my approach to his cottage, he had been out of work.

On entering, I found Mrs. Howland in a pretty considerable fume. Apparently she had worked herself into a heat of temper, which, perhaps, was not altogether unaccountable, even if inexcusable, by reason of her husband being seated near the window, with a book open before him.

"I am glad you are come in, sir," said the wife. "Look at Howland, sitting there, reading half the time, and nothing in the house to eat but what I get in debt for. And I wonder the baker trusts us, that I do."

"My dear," said the husband, who had before accosted me, and was now standing with his hand on the book he had been reading, "the Lord will provide. I am not a bit afraid of help not coming." He said this very mildly, and I must give him the credit of having borne his wife's scolding with meekness.

"Yes, sir, and that's how he goes on," said Mrs. Howland, almost crying. "When I tell him that there isn't a bit of victuals in the cupboard, all I can get from him is, 'The Lord will provide;' and 'tis so with other things,——there's rent not paid, and children's clothes and shoes wearing out; and 'tis all the same cry, 'The Lord will provide,' or 'Cast your burden upon the Lord,' or something of that sort out of the Bible. I declare it is enough to provoke a saint."

"Gently, gently, my good friend," said I, as persuasively as I could. "I am sure you do not mean to disparage the Bible. You have found it before now a great relief in time of trouble, have you not?"

I had reason for saying this, knowing as I do that my poor friend, Martha Howland, notwithstanding a little infirmity of temper, was a truly Christian woman.

"Yes," said she, "I have found it to be so; but————"; and coming to the "but," she stopped short. "Only it does not seem to me right, anyhow, for a man to be sitting in doors half the day, reading the Bible even, when he ought to be looking out for work to keep his family."

"My Martha is something like another Martha we read of in this book," said William Howland, patting his Bible fondly, and speaking kindly, though with a kind of provoking coolness, as I thought; "she is troubled about many things, not that she does not attend to the one thing needful; I don't say that," he added.

"And I reckon if Martha's sister Mary had had a family of little children to look after, and no money coming in, she would have been troubled about many things too," retorted Mrs. Howland.

"Well, to leave these matters now," said I, as I thought that if peacemakers are to be blessed, they have sometimes a delicate and dangerous task to perform, "I have a little job for you, Howland, which will bring you in a shilling. Will you take this letter for me to ————— (I produced the letter and mentioned the place, about three miles off), and wait for an answer?"

To be sure he would, and be glad to oblige me, he said.

I thought, but did not say, that possibly I was obliging him by offering him a shilling for what the postman or the post-office would have done for a penny. The truth is, I knew how badly off my neighbours were, and was glad of an opportunity of putting a shilling in their way without making a show of charity. I could have given the shilling without exacting a return; but it was my whim at that time to make the man fairly earn it, so I only said, "Bring the answer to my house, William, and then I will pay you for the journey."

"Shall I go at once, sir?" he wanted to know.

I told him yes; and so he shut up the book, and took his departure, leaving me in his cottage.

"Did you ever see the like of Will?" said Martha, whose wrath was not yet subsided.

"There are many worse husbands than Will," I replied.

"I don't complain of him as a husband altogether," continued she; "but it isn't much of a husband's part either, when he won't look out for work as he ought, and won't try to keep it when he has got it."

"You have told him so, I have no doubt."

"Haven't I, sir? I just have. I have been giving him such a dressing!"

"I thought so. Now do you think that was quite wise, Mrs. Howland?" I asked.

"I don't know what to say about that, sir; but one can't be always wise, you know, when things go so uncommonly crooked."

"But, my good friend, you know where it is written, 'The Lord layeth up sound wisdom for the righteous;' and you being one of that class————"

"No, no, sir; I never set up for being righteous," said my neighbour, hastily.

"I am sure of that," said I. "If you had done so, it would only have been self-righteousness. What I understand by the righteous, in the highest sense, is those who are made so by the righteousness of Christ; and if any one might be expected to have sound wisdom laid up for them, I am sure they have a right to it. Now, you trust in the Lord Jesus Christ; then you are made righteous in Him. Don't you know where it is written, 'Not having mine own righteousness, which is of the law, but that which is through the faith of Christ, the righteousness which is of God by faith'?"

Yes, my neighbour knew this; it was a great comfort to her to know something of the meaning of it, she said.

"Well, then, to come to the point from which we have started, being a Christian woman, your husband, your children, I, everybody, have a sort of right to expect from you the fruits of that wisdom which cometh from above; and, as you know, is 'first pure, then peaceable, gentle, and easy to be intreated.'"

"To be sure, sir, there's no doubt of that. But, you see, when a poor woman, whether Christian or not, is hard pushed, and the husband won't do what he ought, why, then maybe she forgets what she ought to remember, and wisdom, as you call it, sir, is just nowhere."

"'If any of you lack wisdom,' said the apostle James, 'let him (or her) ask of God, who giveth to all liberally, and upbraideth not.' There are two lessons for us there, I think," said I.

"Very likely," said Martha; "and I want teaching badly enough."

"The first lesson is the plain one, that when we are in a sort of trouble we should go to God, through the Lord Jesus Christ, for guidance. The next is, that if God does not upbraid us for our folly, we should take care how we set about upbraiding others."

"And that's true," said Martha; "I never thought of that before."

"And then," I continued, "the Bible, especially the new Testament part of it, clearly sets before us our Christian duty, whatever may be our station and position in life. You know what it says about wives; but I don't think that it is anywhere said, 'Wives, scold your husbands.'"

Mrs. Howland smiled at this. "A funny thing that would be if it did," said she.

"But something is said about the husband being the head of the wife."

Martha remembered this, and thought that no good was likely to come by her scolding her husband, as she acknowledged she had done.

"Certainly no good can come of it, because it is contrary to the law and the gospel."

"But what is a poor wife to do?" asked Martha, in much perplexity; "you don't think it is right for Will to be hanging about indoors all day, or pretty near it, when he ought to be at work, or looking after it——though it is the Bible he is reading?"

"No; I do not. There is a time for all things, and——but I am not going to talk to you about your husband, that wouldn't be fair. Leave him to me; I'll talk to him."

"I'd be thankful to you, sir, if you would," said Martha.

"Only you must promise me not to scold him again, nor yet to upbraid him (that's the word, you know) about anything past and gone. Because, in the first place, it does no good, as you acknowledge; and in the second place it is neither wise nor right. The Christian rule is, 'Be ye kind one to another, tender-hearted, forgiving one another, even as God, for Christ's sake, hath forgiven you.' Now, as it seems that scolding does not move your husband, why not try another plan? Let me tell you a fable.

"Once upon a time there was a dispute between the sun and the wind which had the most power. They agreed to test the question upon a traveller on the road, who was wrapped in a cloak. 'I'll blow the cloak off his back,' said the wind. 'No, you won't; but I'll make him throw it off,' said the sun. Now, we will call the wind by the name of Anger, and the sun shall be Kindness; the man's cloak being Idleness or Self-indulgence. Well, the wind began to blow with all its might, and gave the traveller a terrible scolding, so to speak; but it only made him draw the cloak all the closer about him. Then, when the wind had done its best, or its worst, and had not succeeded, came out the sun, and presently it sent down such warm rays (of kindness, you understand) that the traveller could not stand it any longer, but threw off his cloak. So the sun beat."

"Well, I never!"

"You try it," said I.

THE FOOL AND THE BARON.

n one of the baronial halls of England lived Harold, a celebrated jester. He was a faithful servant, and a great favourite in the family. His master was so pleased with his drollery that on one occasion he gave him a white wand, saying, "There, Harold, keep that as your staff of office, till you find a greater fool than yourself, and then you may give it to him."

The wand was henceforth Harold's companion; and as years passed by he still made fun, and was still high in favour. At length his master was ill, and there was gloom on every countenance. People passed hither and thither, and spoke in a whisper, and the whisper was, "He is going to die." At last the servants were sent for to take their leave; and Harold, who, averse to sorrow, had hid himself away, was sought out and conducted to the turret chamber to say a final good-bye to his lord.

"Ill, my noble master?"

"Yes, Harold! I'm going on a long journey."

"Where, cousin?"

"I do not know."

"When, most noble?"

"I cannot say."

"When will it please you to return, my lord?"

"Never."

"Will you take poor Harold with you?"

"I must go alone."

"Have you prepared for this sudden journey?"

"No; I knew of it long ago, but I put it off."

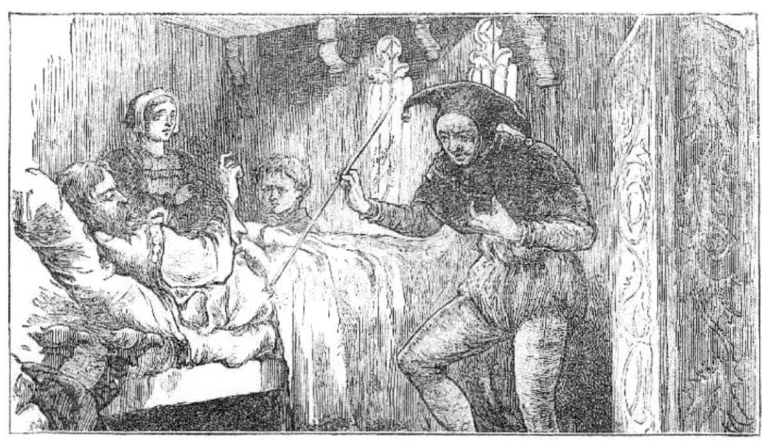

"Why, now," said the jester, "here is a wise thing! You go a journey——so long, so soon; you know not when nor where; you go alone; you will never return: and you have not made ready, though you were told! There, poor noble cousin! take with thee Harold's wand; for in truth this day thou hast found for him a greater fool than himself."

What the fool said to his master was perfectly true, although told in a quaint, blunt style. It suggests some thoughts and reminds us of certain facts which we shall do well to think about.

We shall all have to go on a journey soon. You and I, my friend, must be such travellers as the jester and his master talked of. The journey of death we must each take. What a mysterious journey it is! There are certain roads that we know quite well. So frequently have we travelled them, that we are perfectly familiar with them. The houses we have to pass have an old look. We recognise each field through which we pass. Even many of the trees under whose shade we walk are distinctly remembered by us from time to time. But how different is it with the last road along which we shall travel! None of us know it. It is enshrouded in darkness. We shall travel it for the first as well as for the last time; and those who have trodden it have sent no message to tell us about it.

And this journey is unavoidable. Many journeys are a matter of choice. We can either take them or remain at home. But it is not so with the pilgrimage of death. "It is appointed unto men once to die." Reader, remember this. Do not, like many, try to banish the thought of death from your mind. The last day must come to you. Putting death out of your thoughts will not put it out of existence. Forgetfulness of it cannot destroy it. Since, then, death must come, let us, like wise men, look it full in the face. Let us think solemnly about it.

But to return to the story with which we set out. The jester asked the nobleman if he were prepared for the journey which he was about to take. All journeys require preparation. No one thinks of taking a journey without making ready beforehand; we think the matter well over, find out what we shall need, and provide accordingly. Before the Asiatic traveller mounts the camel which is to bear him across the hot, sandy, dreary wilderness, he takes care to fill his wallet with food and his leathern bottles with water. When the adventurer resolves to make his way through Indian jungles where the tiger lurks, he shoulders his gun, and takes with him a native guide. The wary explorer, ere he steps into his reindeer sledge to cross the ice-bound rivers and snow-clad plains of Arctic regions, arms himself well against the intense cold.

But how shall you prepare for this journey? You are by nature a lost and ruined sinner. You have broken God's commands in your heart and in your daily life; your transgressions are numberless. You cannot change your own heart, and you cannot blot out your own sins. You can of yourself make no preparation for the journey you are about to take; you can do nothing to make yourself meet for God's presence. So far as you are concerned, the words must stand: "Your iniquities have separated between you and your God, and your sins have hid His face from you" (Isa. lix. 2). To provide for your helpless condition, God, in tender love and compassion, gave His only begotten Son, that He should "die for your sins, and rise again for your justification." Is it, then, the language of your broken and contrite heart, "What must I do to be saved? How shall I prepare to meet God?" God's gracious reply is plain and simple: "Believe on the Lord Jesus Christ, and thou shalt be saved." Yes, the blood of Christ shall cleanse you from all unrighteousness, shall justify you freely and fully before God.

But perhaps you say, "I have not that broken heart, and I lack that saving faith." Then may God by His Spirit apply these words powerfully to your heart: "Him hath God exalted with his right hand to be a Prince and a Saviour, for to give repentance to Israel, and forgiveness of sins" (Acts v. 31). All you need is the Saviour's precious gift, and He waits to be gracious. "Ask, and it shall be given you."

Thus faith in Christ will make you ready for the last and solemn journey. It will give you pardon and peace; it will sanctify your heart and life; it will enable you to say with happy assurance, "Yea, though I walk through the valley of the shadow of death, I will fear no evil; for Thou art with me; Thy rod and Thy staff they comfort me."

THE TAILOR'S SPEECH.

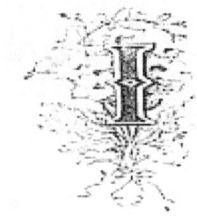

t was in the kitchen of the "Fighting Cocks," a house noted for strong ale, that young Hatfield, a poor ailing journeyman tailor, was haranguing his drinking companions. His face was a little heated by what he had drunk, his hat was dented in as though it had been used for a football, and the elbow of his right arm, as he lifted up his pipe, was seen through his ragged sleeve.

It happened that old Cawthorn, a staid and respectable servant, who lived in the neighbourhood, had a note to deliver at the bar, and the landlord of the "Fighting Cocks" being out of the way, old Cawthorn stood waiting for him, while young Hatfield "laid down the law" to his companions. As he proceeded, old Cawthorn, who well knew the bad habits of the speaker, kept talking to himself in reply to the observations made.

"I have seen a great deal of life, my friends," said the tailor.

"And sad low life, too, I am afraid."

"If people would only be ruled by me————"

"Ay, but bad as things are, we are not come to such a pass as that yet."

"If people would only be ruled by me, old England would lift up her head again. In the first place I would reform the constitution."

"Beginning with your own, I hope, for that seems not to be over excellent. What next, I wonder!"

"There should be no places and pensions; no bribery and corruption; no taxes and oppression; but every man should have his rights, and a poor man should lift up his head as well as a rich man."

"If you could only rule yourself as well as you think you could rule the nation, it would at any rate be a good beginning."

"I would inclose all the waste lands in England, every one of them should be cultivated."

"Better by half weed your own little garden first, for it is sadly out of order."

"Every man's house, ay, the poorest among them, should have in it a flitch of good bacon."

"That is more than is ever likely to be found in yours, Master Hatfield, unless you live a very different life to what you now do."

"I have a notion that we might all of us live much happier than we now do, and with half the labour."

"A notion, indeed, and nothing but a notion. But if you paid a little less attention to the country at large, and a little more to your own habits, you and your poor wife and little ones might live happier than you do, there is little doubt."

"We seem to be all wrong in religious matters. Instead of being brought up to particular opinions, every one, young and old, ought to be left at liberty to think as he pleases."

"And to do as he pleases, too, I suppose? Oh! Harry Hatfield. Some day or other, if you keep a little closer to your shopboard, you may shine as a tailor, but you are not likely to become a star in any other calling."

"Then with regard to property; it stands to reason that if the hundred thousand pounds possessed by the rich man were to be divided into a hundred parts, it would make a hundred men comfortable and happy instead of one."

"All housebreakers and highwaymen, I should think, reason in the same way."

"It costs the country millions a year to keep up the gaols and the policemen: every penny of this might be saved."

"Ay, and the land might be overrun with rogues, and the country become a bear-garden."

"The national debt ought to be wiped away at once——it is a disgrace to the nation."

"And there is a debt scored up on the door there that is a disgrace to one Harry Hatfield——I suppose you would wipe that away too."

"In a word, my friends, things are very different to what they ought to be. In this land of liberty, where every man's house is his castle, and where everything should be properly conducted, there ought to be no policemen——no oppressive laws——no taxes——no————"

Here the landlord made his appearance, and old Cawthorn, having delivered his note, left the house, saying, "How true is that proverb of Solomon, 'Seest thou a man wise in his own conceit? there is more hope of a fool than of him.'"

NOT A BIT AFRAID.

es, I know it's a serious case; the doctor said so. But I don't trouble myself about that; I'm not a bit afraid."

"But you told me just now that you had not attended to religion a great deal. You know this is the first time I ever saw you; so I know nothing about you but what you tell me. I suppose, in fact, you have lived like many more, without much thought about your soul?"

"Yes, sir, that's it."

"And yet you are not afraid?"

"No, sir, I don't feel afraid at all. I'm not troubled in my mind. I have been no wise wicked."

The minister looked grave.

"You mean you have not been a thief, or a great drinker, or a swearer, or a liar, or anything of that sort?"

"No, no; I have not been anything of the kind. I know plenty who have; but I've always tried to live respectable."

"Well, but do you mean to say you are not a sinner?"

"Oh, we are all sinners, of course."

"But does not that mean anything? Does it not *signify* being a sinner?"

"I've never done anything bad in particular, as I know of. At all events, I don't feel afraid."

"I wish you did," said the minister earnestly; "I wish you did with all my heart. I know *I* should if I were you."

The sick man looked surprised; but he made no answer, so the minister went on.

"As for me, I could not speak as you do. I know that I am a poor sinner; and that, but for my Saviour, I must be lost for ever. But I have gone to Him, and sought His blood to wash away my sins, and I do humbly believe in Him; and He, and He alone, takes *my* fear away. You have told me what *you* feel, and now I have told you what *I* feel."

"Well, that's all right, sir, no doubt," was all the sick man said. The minister went on again:

"Oh, my friend, it will never do to say you are not afraid while you have not gone to Christ; you ought to be afraid, you have good reason to be afraid. I *must* be plain with you. I dare not build you up with false hopes. Don't you know that you must stand before God, and give account for all your life? Don't you know about the great judgment day, when the books will be opened? These books will have in them all you have ever done in your life. Can you face that? Are you not afraid when you think of *that*? There will be another book opened then, the book of life. That will contain the names of all who are saved by Jesus Christ. And everybody else (do you remember that?) will be cast into the lake of fire. You know you have not lived to God, you know you have not sought Christ, your religion has been nothing but a name; and, say what you will, you know quite well that you have often and often done wrong. Now, how *can* you say you are not afraid?"

The man shifted uneasily on his bed.

"Perhaps," said he, "I ought to be more afraid than I am."

"Yes, indeed you ought. I don't want to give you pain, I want to comfort you; but I dare not give you false comfort. I want you to see the *truth*. You are a poor sinner in need of a Saviour. You may think lightly of your sins now, and hardly call them sins at all; but if you saw them as they really are, oh how black they would look to you! I pray God to teach you to see *yourself*, and to see your sins, *now*, before the books are opened. And now let me speak to you about Jesus Christ. He pitied us poor sinners, and came and died on the cross to save us. Thousands have been saved by Him. He has never turned *one* away who went to Him for salvation. I hope I have gone. I *know* I have. I could not rest in my bed if I had not. I want *you* to go to Him too. He calls you to Him. Just as you are, He bids you look to Him and be saved. He is willing to be your Saviour. *Now*, remember, *now*, He is willing to be your Saviour.

Do not put this off. Sometimes people put away such thoughts because they trouble them. Oh, do not *you* do so. Here you are alone on your bed away from everybody. Now *pray*, pray for the Holy Spirit to teach your heart, pray that Jesus may be your Saviour. Let me pray with you before I go."

And the minister knelt down and prayed. And when he rose from his knees, the sick man held out his hand, and his eyes were wet with tears, and he did not say again that he was not afraid; but he said in a low voice, "I hope God will forgive me. You'll come and see me again, sir?"

TOLD AT A TUNNEL'S MOUTH.

group of navvies waited for the relief party at the mouth of a tunnel.

"Sing us a song, Sam!" said one.

"Got a cold, Bill; try the new hand."

A loud laugh followed this remark, and that for two reasons; one was Sam's cold, which was not strange, seeing that for fourteen hours they had worked (as only English navvies can) in that long tunnel, at times half choked with smoke and steam, and then half-frozen with the bitter winter wind; the other reason was his suggestion for the fresh hand to sing, whose strange silent manner had not made him a favourite in the rough but hearty gang of navvies. Once Sam had watched and saw him reach over a part of his dinner to a mate who was "not up to the mark," when the said mate could not swallow the hard fare he had provided himself with; and Sam wished to know more, being, as he would have said, "kinder curus on sich p'ints," so he asked.

"P'rhaps you'll oblige?"

"How long have we got, mates?"

"Matter of half-hour before the relief comes."

"I'll sing you a song at last, if you'll hear a story first."

"Hear! hear!" said Sam; and the rest agreed. So the new hand placed himself a little nearer the middle of the group, and leaning on his pick, began:

"A bargain is a bargain, mates, and I shall keep you to your word; if you don't hear me out——no song. I'm going to talk about my little Meg; and if you don't know why I am quiet-like now, you will before I have done. Once I had as nice a home as any man need wish for, and the girl I brought to it was the right sort, I can tell you; none of your flashy, dressy, empty-headed ones, but a right down decent hard-working maid she was. But she was religious, always wanted to go to church or chapel, or what not, on the Sunday, and I didn't care for that; so I told her, 'Alice,' says I, 'you have married me, and you'll have to stick to me, or else there'll be a row.' Well, she begged to go, but I would not hear a word of it; so she gave in.

"So we went on for more than a year; I was middlin' steady, and she kept the home up well, only I noticed she seemed less happy-like; and if I stopped her going to church or chapel on Sunday, I couldn't get her to go out for pleasure with me; for she said, 'Fair's fair; I keep away from one place to please you, I keep away from others to please myself.' And I thought there was something in that; don't you?"

The men made a murmur, half yes, half no, and seemed to grow more attentive; it was level with their understanding.

He went on.

"Soon after that Meg was born, and how glad Alice was, to be sure! why, that child, I believe she would have worked her fingers to the bone for it. Some folks talk as if our little ones were a curse to us; why, mates, them as says so are worse than a jackdaw, and as empty as a bag of wind; they ain't got no heart themselves."

"No; they're all jaw," said Sam.

"Well, anyway, we didn't call Meg a curse by a long stretch; she crowed and grew, and every year bound us more together; for whatever little differences we had in other things we were one on the babe——she was the best in the world. But while Meg grew strong the mother grew weak, until she was as thin as a shadow; then I asked the doctor, who said she wanted change of air. I asked her if she would like to go and see her mother, and take Meg; lor', how pleased she was! So she went, and I saw her off.

"How I got on without her I don't know; badly enough it was. When she came back little Meg was four years old. Mates, I didn't know the wife, so white and ill she was; but the child was brighter than ever, the sunshine of our lives. To make the story short, while I hoped and hoped Alice would mend, she didn't; and the sight of her face, so ghost-like, kind of haunted me——she was queer and lonely-like and—— well, lads, I took to drink!"

The fresh hand's voice quivered a little, but he grasped the pick firmer, and continued: "Most every night I kept away from home, not because I hated it, boys, for my heart was there, but I just could not bear to see Alice; somehow death appeared written in her face, and I wanted to give him plenty of room——I was not ready for him. The neighbours kept the place and Meg tidy, and I took home what was left after paying score at the 'Lion.'"

Bill gave Sam a good nudge to look at the speaker, for the tears had gathered in his eyes and were rolling in little channels down his cheeks.

"One night there was a noise in the bar at the 'Lion.' Somebody sung out, 'Mind the little 'un;' then there was a fall and a cry——Meg's cry——and I ran out, to see the landlady catch her up, and the blood flowing from a great gash in the forehead. 'Pure accident,' some one said; but I caught hold of Meg, the landlady bound her up somehow, and I rushed home with her——home to her mother, and the sight of the child seemed to put life into Alice; she fondled and sang to the little one in a way that almost broke my heart. The doctor came and bound the head up, but the little eyes were fast closed and he gave no hope.

"Once she opened the little eyes, gave one stare wild enough to shudder at, and then closed them; so we sat, Alice with her on her breast in bed, and I on a chair by the side.

"'John,' said Alice, 'I don't think I shall be here long, and I want to talk to you a bit; will you listen?'

"I nodded, for I could not speak.

"'Before I knew you, John, I used to read my Bible and pray to God; since then I have given it up; you did not like it, John; but I have got to die; and it's all dark now, husband. What am I to do?'

"I kept quite still; what could I say?

"'John, I'm too weak to read now; won't you read a bit to me, and give me a little comfort before I die——if there is any for me?'

"Not for years had I touched the book she spoke of, and where to find it now I did not know; but I hunted round, for I thought, if this will give her ease, I'm bound to try; and at last I found it behind the tea-tray. I asked her where to read; she said anywhere. So I opened and read where Jesus went into a house in which a little child lay dead; how the people mocked and jeered Him when He said she slept (and I looked at our poor Meg, so white and pained, wondering if He would have come to her); how Jesus took that little girl's hand, her cold, dead hand, and said, 'Arise.'

"'Oh, John, if He were only here to speak to Meg and make her well!' said Alice.

"'Perhaps it's only a tale,' I said——and stopped.

"'No, John,' said Alice. 'When I was well I could live and not think much of Him; but since I've been ill He seems very real to me sometimes; even now, John, I believe He is here!'

"Mates, that was a cold, dark night, and the wind howled outside, the fire was all but out, and the candle flickered about with the draught. I tell you I felt bad, for her words did seem so full of meaning, her eyes almost looked me through.

"'John, if He's here, He can save our Meg. John dear, won't you ask Him? Won't you pray?'

"'Alice, I can't; I don't know how.'

"'Husband, look at the darling; think of her——of her! John, try. Oh, John, try!'"

The whole group of navvies gathered round him here with open eyes and strained ears, watching eagerly for what was coming.

"I don't know what voice whispered back her words like an echo; but I heard, and fell upon my knees crying to the Lord——if He was there——to have mercy on my sinful soul, and to heal our little lamb. Oh, mates, how I did cry, to be sure! and how I did hope it might be true that He was there! for I felt sure, if He was, He would help us——the old story I had learned years before and forgotten so long——the story of His cruel death, seemed to rise like a strange bright picture in the awful stillness of that room: how He died for *sinners*, that such might be brought back to God——this broke down my hardened heart. Just then, whilst I was on my knees, and the tears of penitence were on my cheeks, Meg, dear little Meg, opened her eyes once more. 'Oh, father, I have had such a beautiful dream,' she said; 'the Lord whom mammy loves has come, and called to such a lovely house your poor tired Meg. Father, take care of dear mammy!'

"The little eyes grew more weary, closed at last, and with one long sigh Meg was gone to the lovely home."

The rough men were touched indeed as he stopped to gasp down his emotion.

"Lads, the mother went before long, clinging to the Lord whom Meg saw, resting on His word as she passed through the Valley of the Shadow into the Light beyond. The old place was too full of sorrow for me; so I wandered on till I got to this place; and if I'm quiet, it is because I think of them. Ever as I work the sense of His presence is with me; their dying words are in my ears. Oh! mates, take my story home to your hearts——home to your wives and little ones, and with them seek the Saviour, whose love so strangely made me turn from evil unto God."

Not a word had interrupted him all through; but now Sam's voice was heard but little above a whisper,

"Mate, we want the song."

John cleared his voice a little, and, as the men hushed down again, sang:——

"I stay a little while below;

The changing seasons come and go,

But Christ my joy heals every woe,

In Him I live and fear no foe.

"The night is dark and sad to me,

But even in the gloom I see

My Saviour bright who died to free

My soul from misery.

"Though He has taken those above

Who once have cheered me with their love,

Clad in the robe His hands have wove,

They safely rest, where'er I rove.

"So still to Him my steps do tend;

His power is present to defend;

On His sweet mercy I depend;

His love to me will never end.

"Friends, come to Him, just as you are;

His arms of mercy reach as far

As ever son of man can need;

His blood can pardon, and His love can feed."

HARVEST HOME.

o and stand on the hill yonder, and look round. What do you see? Gold here——gold there——gold everywhere!

All so busy——so earnest.

"How is Mr. Sharp's barley?" says one. "How will Mr. Bell's wheat turn out, think you?" says another. "Oh," cries a third, "if the fine weather does but hold we shall do well. It was a very good change of the moon, and I hope to get in my bit in safety."

The trouble is to get labourers. When there is no work about there is plenty of grumbling among labourers; and no wonder, for if they don't work, how can they eat? and when there is abundance of work there is plenty of grumbling among employers; and no wonder, for if hands are so scarce, and wages run so high, that it is almost impossible to house the grain and seed in time, where is the rent to come from? Well, this is a world where grumbling is to be looked for, but there is a harvest coming at the close of it when all murmurs, all cares, will be done away; when the reapers, who will be the holy angels, will be enough for their work, and when no fear that a single grain of good seed will perish, but all will be safely gathered into the heavenly garner.

Now, here is a true story, though the names of the people are not given, because they are yet alive; very likely they may see this, and if they do, they will exclaim, "Oh, yes; this is true indeed!"

There was a great revival of religion in a certain parish; many persons who had lived in utter deadness as to God and a world to come were awakened out of their sleep, and wept and prayed earnestly for faith to the saving of their souls. The picture of the great Harvest Home was brought before them with such power that they felt nothing was of consequence compared with the question of their being among the tares or the wheat.

A lady, who was staying there on a visit, was much touched by what she saw around her, and especially interested in one woman, who gave proof that her repentance was sincere, and her faith a living faith.

She often thought of this poor woman——for she was very poor——after her return home; and having met with a book which she thought would give comfort and encouragement, she put it by, determining to send it some time. But "some time" did not satisfy her, she had so strong a desire to do it at once, that she folded it up to post it. Still, she was not satisfied——what more had she to do? It came into her mind, "Put in half-a-crown; she is very poor, and it will be a help to her." So she put in the half-crown, directed the parcel plainly and fully, and put it in the post. The postman next day duly delivered the packet to the woman. "Oh," she said, not opening it, "this must be a mistake, I don't know anybody that would send a book to me. You had best inquire who expected one" (perhaps there were others of her name in the place, but this I do not know). The postman recommended her to open it and see if she could make out that it was hers, he would inquire on his return if she still said it was not.

With the parcel in her hand she met a neighbour who, like herself, now feared the Lord and lived in prayer. "What have you there?" she said. "Oh, it's a parcel that must have come by mistake," she replied. "I know nobody away from home——and look!" she exclaimed as she untied the paper and the half-crown dropped out. They consulted together, and wondered much who it could be that had sent it; but guessed wrong altogether, and made sure they had done so. At length the neighbour said, "Have you been asking the Lord for anything lately?" "No, nothing particular, except it was for the money to pay my club that is due to-day, and if I don't pay in I am forfeit, you know!" "Good, now," said the neighbour; "don't you see who has sent it? Why, the Lord, to be sure. He heard your prayer, and knew it was just what you wanted; so He put it into some Christian heart to send it. Go and pay it in (it was just the money), and give Him the thanks."

Now, see what it is to be one of the grains of wheat that are to be gathered into His garner! When the harvest comes the angels will look after the very smallest, and not only so, but till then the very smallest and meanest will be kept and cared for and ministering spirits, either of their fellow Christians (like this lady) or those blessed creatures who, we are told, "are sent forth to minister to the heirs of salvation," will be employed by their Saviour to help them in every need.

"Ah! but I have seen Christians left a long time in great trouble," says one. "So have I," says another. Have you? Well, be sure of this, while God's word stands true it must have been that they neglected fervent prayer to be helped out of it; or else their remaining in trouble was for their good in the end; for it is written, "All things whatsoever ye shall ask in prayer, believing, ye shall receive," and it is written also, "No good thing will He withhold from them that walk uprightly."

A gentleman who farmed his own land and was known to treat his labourers well had a company of Irishmen every year——year after year, who came to work all through the harvest. They were very sober, clean, hard-working, and well conducted; so that they were allowed to sleep in a barn, and had the use of a fire in the back kitchen to boil their milk (which was given them) and their potatoes. They felt quite at home when they got to this estate, and had as much confidence in the kindness of their employers as they had in them.

One day one of them, Paddy Brady, asked to see the lady of the house. She was a most benevolent woman, and took a lively interest in these Irish reapers. Paddy, making his most genteel bow (she used to say they were quite gentlemen in their manners), asked her if she would be so obliging as to direct a letter for him.

"Surely, Paddy, I will," she answered, "but if you can write a whole letter yourself, why can't you direct it?"

"Sure, it's another thing quite," said Paddy. "Biddy Brady, my wife, knows me so well she can read the inside as plain as if I was speaking; but there's never a one of the men as'll carry it across the water as has got the least bit of notion of me, and how can they read my writing, so strong of the brogue?"

The lady couldn't see the wisdom of this reason, but she didn't like to interfere with Paddy's view, and he was satisfied with it. So, though she laughed to herself, the letter was directed according to his desire.

"And now, my lady, if you'd just do me the favour to give me one of them things to put in the corner, I'll pay you for it and thank you all the same as if you gave it out of your free generosity," said Paddy, who looked with admiration at the direction, which, however, would have given him more trouble to read than his own writing——"so strong of the brogue" within.

The lady took a Queen's head and put it on the letter, refusing the penny. "Put by the penny," she said, "you will have that much more to carry home to your wife."

"God bless you, my lady! I hope I'll have to work for you many years yet; and beyant all and everything I hope we'll both get good luck in the grand harvest that's to come at the end!"

His eyes were full of grateful feeling as he spoke, and she was, as you will believe, much touched with his simple earnestness.

There was everything in Paddy's wish. Whether he knew anything of the Lord of the harvest, and, in spite of ignorance and the false teaching of his priest, looked for His coming with hope and love, I cannot say; but certain it is, to be under the care of the angel reapers there, instead of being left to the winds of destruction, should be every one's chief concern.

End of the book.